The
Asian Tsunami
2004

A Huge Wave Kills Thousands

JOHN TOWNSEND

CHICAGO, ILLINOIS

Customer Service 888-363-4266
Visit our website at www.heinemannraintree.com

Designed by Victoria Bevan and AMR Design Ltd
Illustrations by David Woodroffe
Printed and bound in China by South China Printing Company

10 09 08 07 06
10 9 8 7 6 5 4 3 2 1

Library of Congress Cataloging-in-Publication Data
Townsend, John, 1955-
  The Indian Ocean tsunami 2004 / John Townsend.
    p. cm. -- (When disaster struck)
  Includes bibliographical references and index.
  ISBN 1-4109-2277-4 (library binding)
  1. Indian Ocean Tsunami, 2004--Juvenile literature. 2. Tsunamis--Indian Ocean--Juvenile literature. I. Title. II. Series.

  GC221.5T69 2006
  909'.09824083--dc22

                    2005034638

Acknowledgments
The publishers would like to thank the following for permission to reproduce photographs:
Alamy Images p. 11 (Leisa Hale); Corbis pp. 9 (NEWS LTD/AUSTRAL), 20 (Babu/Reuters), 40); Empics pp. 4 (AP/APTN), 16 (AP/APTN), 19 (AP/Vincent Thian), 24 (AP/Huang Wen Feng, Chief Officer MV Durban Bridge), 25 (AP), 29 (AP/MANISH SWARUP), 35 (AP/WONG MAYE-E), 42 (Bart A Bauer/USN/Abaca/ABACA), 43 (AP/APTN); Getty Images pp. 12 (AFP), 13, 22), 34, 38, 41, 44, 48 (Photodisc); NASA p. 18 (GSFC/Jacques Descloitres, MODIS Land Rapid Response Team); Nature Picture Library p. 47; Rex Features pp. 10 (Eye Ubiquitous), 14 (Digital Globe), 14 (Digital Globe), 33 (Sipa Press), 36 (Sipa Press), 46 (DCY), 49 (Masatoshi Okauchi), Steve Hunter pp. 26), 27); Topham Picturepoint pp. 28 (Zorah/The Image Works), 30 (US Navy/Photographer's Mate 3rd Class Rebecca J. Moat), 32 (Photri/US Navy/Photographer's mate 2nd Class Dennis Cantrell), 37 (US Navy/Photographer's Mate 3rd Class Jacob J. Kirk).

Cover photograph of the tsunami, reproduced with permission of Empics (Eric Skitzi/AP).

The publishers would like to thank Mike Freeman of Samaritan's Purse for his assistance in the preparation of this book.

CONTENTS

Any words appearing in the text in bold, **like this**, are explained in the glossary.

A HUGE WAVE KILLS THOUSANDS

The Asian Tsunami, 2004

FAR BELOW THE SEA

Just before 8:00 A.M. local time on December 26, 2004, the ground shook near Sumatra in Indonesia.

About 150 miles (240 kilometers) off the coast of Sumatra and about 19 miles (30 kilometers) below the ocean floor, an earthquake jolted the seabed for nearly ten minutes. It was one of the most powerful earthquakes ever recorded.

The quake churned up the sea and sent the deadliest waves on record sweeping across the Indian Ocean. Waves reached speeds of 300 miles (480 kilometers) per hour. Waves measuring between 13 and 50 feet (4 and 15 meters) high crashed onto beaches in Indonesia, Thailand, Sri Lanka, and India. Waves even reached Africa, 3,000 miles (4,800 kilometers) away.

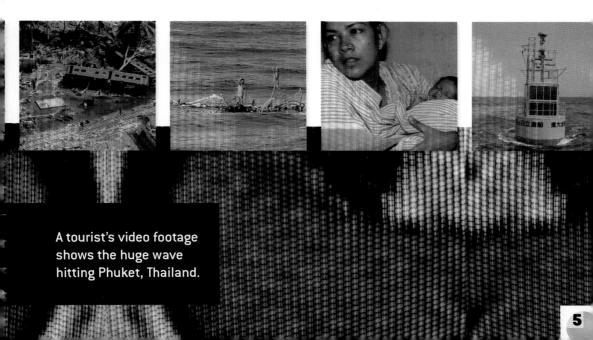

A tourist's video footage shows the huge wave hitting Phuket, Thailand.

WHEN THE WAVE STRUCK

The Asian Tsunami, 2004

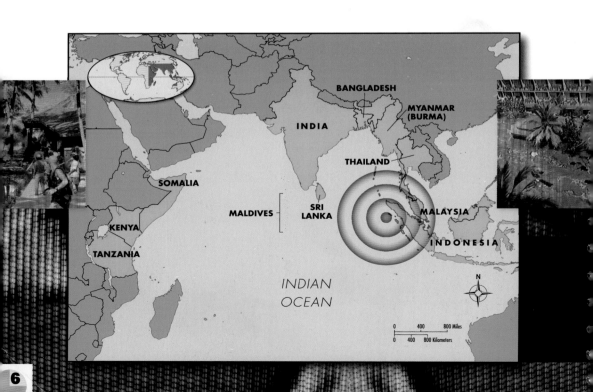

JUST ANOTHER DAY

The morning started as usual for millions of people in countries and islands all around the Indian Ocean.

For many people in Indonesia, that meant farming or fishing near the villages where their families had lived for generations. Traders set out their market stalls in the streets of busy coastal towns. In many **remote** villages along the coast, people lived simply and owned very little. Some people made pots or handmade crafts to sell to tourists.

On the west coast of Thailand, the beach resorts were full with Christmas vacationers. Tourists were swimming, sunbathing, or eating breakfast beneath the palm trees. At 7:59 A.M. scientists at the Pacific Tsunami Warning Center detected a major earthquake in the Indian Ocean. They still had no idea it had triggered a deadly wave.

This map shows where the earthquake took place and the countries affected by the resulting waves.

WHAT WAS KNOWN?

Tsunami is a Japanese word meaning "harbor wave." People living near the sea in many parts of the world have always known about the dangers of tsunamis. Throughout history, tsunamis have struck coasts around parts of the Indian and Pacific oceans. They can happen when Earth's **crust** breaks or moves under the sea. This movement causes giant waves to spread out like huge ripples. The waves can be many feet high and travel huge distances.

Earthquakes often occur near Indonesia, in the Indian Ocean. Here, huge pieces of Earth's crust called **plates** push against each other. Sometimes they move suddenly and cause Earth to shake. Whenever this happens under the sea, a tsunami can form.

THE WORLD'S WORST TSUNAMIS 1994–2003

Date	Place	Reason	Deaths
June 3, 1994	Java, Indonesia	Earthquake	223
February 17, 1996	Biak, Irian Jaya	Earthquake	166
February 21, 1996	Peru	Earthquake	7
November 17, 1996	near Brownsville, Texas	Bad weather	10
July 17, 1998	Papua New Guinea	Earthquake	2,000+
September 15, 1999	Marquesas Islands	Landslide	0

Earthquakes can range from small tremors to massive quakes. Scientists measure the strength of an earthquake and give it a number from 1 to 9 on the **Richter scale**. The earthquake on December 26, 2004, measured 9 on the Richter scale. Scientists knew an enormous earthquake had struck. They could only wait to learn what damage it would cause.

The village of Sissano was destroyed in July 1998 when a tsunami hit Papua New Guinea.

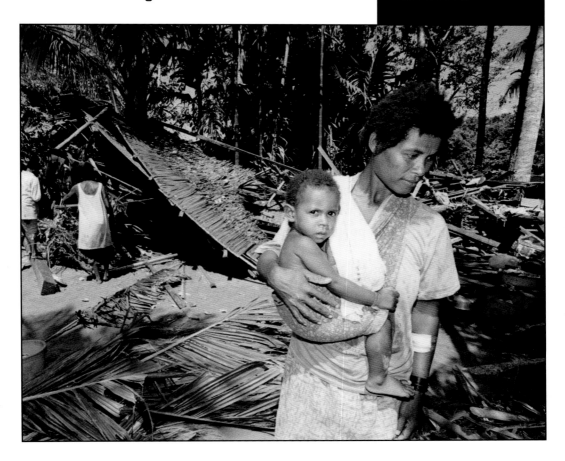

ON THE BEACHES

From many beaches the first sign of the approaching waves was a line of white foam on the **horizon**. At first it seemed like nothing to worry about. Swimmers stood and watched. Fishermen stared from their boats. The waves came nearer and grew larger. In some places, they were more than 65 feet (20 meters) high. Some people began to scream and run. There was chaos as parents tried to gather their children.

On this beach in Thailand, Karin Svaerd ran toward the waves to help her family escape. Miraculously, the whole family survived.

In other places the first sign of anything unusual was the sea appearing to be sucked away, leaving fish stranded on the sand where the water had been. Boats raced for the shore at full speed. People on the beaches turned and ran. Soon, the huge wall of water smashed down on anything in its path.

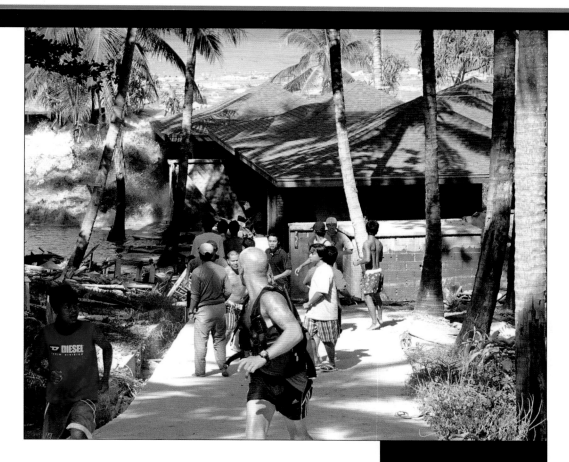

The water rushed up the beaches, crashed into buildings, and poured through streets. The force of the waves destroyed anything in their way.

Many people did not realize how powerful the waves were until it was too late.

DECEMBER 26 TIMELINE

7:59 A.M. local time
(Dec. 25, 7:59 P.M. EST)
Huge earthquake off
the coast of Sumatra

8:30 A.M. local time
(Dec. 25, 8:30 P.M. EST)
Huge waves crash into
Sumatra

9:30 A.M. local time
(Dec. 25, 9:30 P.M. EST)
Waves hit beaches in
southern Thailand

9:00 A.M. local time
(Dec. 25, 10:00 P.M. EST)
Tsunami reaches Sri
Lanka and the coast
of India

9:30 A.M. local time
(Dec. 25, 11:30 P.M. EST)
Tsunami hits the Maldives

10:00 A.M. local time
(Dec. 26, 2:00 A.M. EST)
Tsunami strikes
East Africa

THE FIRST CASUALTIES

The Asian Tsunami, 2004

THE DAMAGE IN INDONESIA

Thousands of people died when the waves hit Sumatra.

The exact number of victims who were drowned or crushed to death by the waves will never be known. Many were washed out to sea. Six months after the disaster, bodies and skeletons were still being found.

About 500,000 Indonesian people were made homeless by the tsunami. They could only take shelter in scattered camps and had to rely on **aid**. Relief organizations said it would take two years to get everyone rehoused.

The Indonesian city of Banda Aceh was one of the worst-hit places. This coastal city was almost totally destroyed, killing thousands of people in just a few minutes.

The satellite photo on the left shows the town of Banda Aceh before the tsunami struck. The photo on the right was taken two days later. The town was almost completely destroyed by the waves.

THE WAVES REACH THAILAND

Thousands of tourists travel to Thailand every year to enjoy the sun, sea, and golden sand. On December 26, 2004, many people were getting up late after Christmas parties the night before. But there were already many swimmers, divers, and sunbathers on the beaches at the resort of Phuket.

Soon after 9:30 A.M. local time, the sea suddenly seemed to change. People described it as moving strangely. A few swimmers screamed as they were sucked out to sea. In the hotels along the beach, people went out on to the balconies to see what was happening. Others rushed to the shoreline. As in Indonesia, it appeared as if the tide had suddenly gone out. Fish lay flapping on the damp sand and already people were picking them up. Rocks in the bay that usually poked just above the water were now towering above the sand.

Hotels along the coast were swamped by the sea.

The popular tourist resort of Phuket was badly damaged by the tsunami.

While everyone wondered what was happening, the sea began to rush back with a roar. The sea surged back at a frightening speed. It crashed up the beach and smashed into the hotels. It washed away chairs and tables from the shore, lifted cars off the road, and hurled them into buildings. It gushed into hotel lobbies, filling rooms with water and **debris**. It poured into basements, swirled up stairways, and broke down doors.

More waves followed, smashing through the streets and knocking down people. Hundreds of shop windows broke as the **torrent** of water burst through them. Now armed with broken glass, the water ripped at people's bodies as they tried to cling to anything they could find.

THE WAVES REACH SRI LANKA

Apart from Indonesia, Sri Lanka suffered more casualties from the tsunami than anywhere else. Its southern coast was torn apart. Crops and fishing boats were flattened and wrecked. More than 100,000 homes were damaged or destroyed, and more than 500,000 people were made homeless.

The tsunami led to one of the worst rail disasters in the world. At Telwatta, in the southwest of Sri Lanka, a train was knocked sideways when the tsunami hit. Up to 1,500 people were crammed inside the train as it traveled from Colombo to Galle.

▶ "EVERYONE VANISHED"

"I was at the Selaka Shopping Center at Galle. There was a great hissing sound from the sea and the sea seemed to be caving in. Within seconds, a great wave came rushing in to the shore, destroying everything. Everyone vanished in a second. The whole town was destroyed in seconds, along with people at the bus stand. It is like a dream. I have never seen anything like it."

Deepa, Galle, Sri Lanka

Coastal areas in the south of Sri Lanka were hit by the waves.

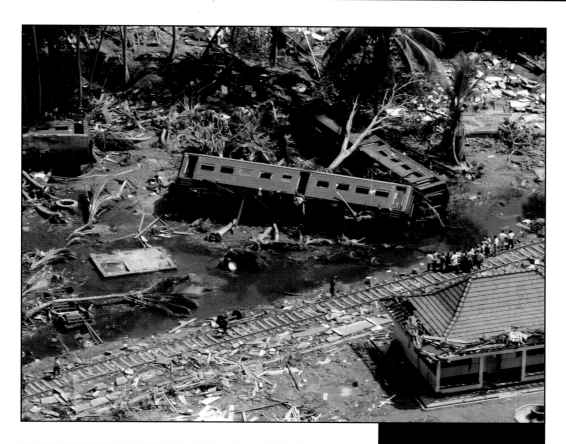

The force of the waves threw the train's eight cars far from the rails.

ESTIMATED 1,000 DEAD ON SRI LANKAN TRAIN

"Police estimated that around 1,000 people were killed when their train, the *Queen of the Sea*, was thrown off the track by this week's raging tsunami. Hundreds of bodies that were pulled from the twisted wreckage were buried Tuesday alongside the railroad line.

The train had come to a stop amid rising waters just before it was struck by the giant wave. Many of the dead were villagers living nearby who tried to escape the waves by climbing onto the top of the train. The force of the waves tore off some of the wheels, and the tracks twisted like a loop on a roller coaster."

The Associated Press, December 29, 2004

THE DAMAGE IN INDIA AND THE MALDIVES

The giant waves spread across the Indian Ocean. Two hours after the earthquake, they reached India. Yet again, people on the beaches were swept away.

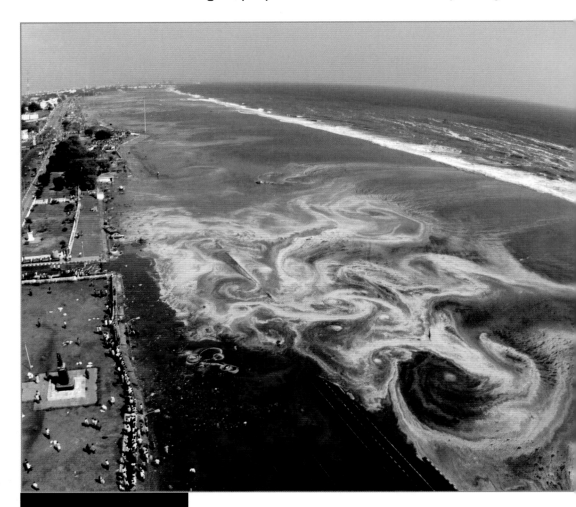

The tsunami swamped the roads at this beach in southern India.

The southeast coast of India was the worst hit, with the sea reaching 2 miles (3 kilometers) inland in places. More than 150,000 homes were destroyed, and over 370 miles (600 kilometers) of roads and fourteen bridges were damaged. The muddy salt water **contaminated** fresh water supplies. Farmland and crops were ruined. Jetties used for getting supplies to the many islands were smashed apart.

The tsunami continued to rush across the Indian Ocean. At 9:30 A.M. local time, it struck the low-lying Maldive Islands. Of the 199 islands, 20 were described as "totally destroyed." Over 4,000 homes were destroyed and about 100 people were killed.

By now, the news of the tsunami was being sent around the world. Very few details were known, but there was enough time to warn countries still in the wave's path. It was heading toward Africa, and it became a race against time to warn people. Some people heard the news and rushed inland, but not everyone received the warning in time.

Between 10:00 and 11.00 A.M. local time, the tsunami hit the coasts of Somalia and Kenya in eastern Africa. It had taken six to seven hours for the waves to travel 3,000 miles (4,800 kilometers) across the Indian Ocean. In May 2005 the Red Cross reported that the tsunami killed 312 people in East Africa (Kenya, Madagascar, Seychelles, Somalia, and Tanzania).

THE CASUALTIES

Indonesia:
130,000 dead
37,000 missing

Thailand:
5,395 dead
2,800 missing

Sri Lanka:
31,000 dead
4,000 missing

India:
11,000 dead

Casualties were also reported in the Maldives, Malaysia, Burma, Bangladesh, Somalia, Kenya, Tanzania, and the Seychelles.

THE LUCKY SURVIVORS

The Asian Tsunami, 2004

AMAZING ESCAPES

News of the disaster spread quickly around the world.

However, it took days before the world knew the full scale of what had happened. No one had realized how many people had been killed, injured, or left homeless. When survivors told of what happened, the world was stunned. Newspapers were full of survivors' stories. Some were about people who just happened to be in the right place at the right time and escaped being washed away. Others were about people who ran to safety, like the ten-year-old British girl who remembered her geography class about tsunamis. When she saw the water disappearing from a beach in Thailand, she told her family to run away just before the waves came back.

There were amazing stories of fishermen surviving at sea for days in smashed boats. Among all the tragic stories, there were amazing accounts of survival.

These four fishermen from Sumatra were rescued by helicopter after the tsunami smashed their boat. They drifted for nine days in a dinghy with no food or water.

DAYS AT SEA

No one will ever know how many thousands of people were dragged out to sea by the retreating waves. The chances of anyone surviving long in the Indian Ocean were low. Yet there were some amazing stories about survivors.

Rizal Shahputra was 23 and cleaning a **mosque** in Aceh province, Sumatra, when the tsunami hit. "Everybody sank; my family sank. There were bodies around me," he said. He grabbed onto an uprooted palm tree and was swept out to sea. He clung on for eight days as currents took him 100 miles (160 kilometers) out into the ocean. He stayed alive by drinking rainwater and eating coconuts from the palm tree. At last he saw a ship in the distance and waved to it. One of the crew saw Rizal and the ship picked him up. He was taken to a hospital in Malaysia. Amazingly Rizal only had minor injuries.

Spotted by sailors on a Japanese ship, Rizal Shahputra was taken to neighboring Malaysia.

Another 23-year-old from Aceh had a lucky escape. Her name was Melawati and she, too, was swept out to sea, where she was adrift for days.

Melawati had seen sharks circling her raft while she was adrift.

WOMAN SAVED FROM WAVES

"A Malaysian tuna ship rescued a woman who had drifted for five days in the Indian Ocean. Last week's tsunami swept her out to sea from her home on Sumatra island.

Melawati was spotted alive and clinging to an uprooted palm tree. She had leg injuries as a result of being bitten by fish. She was very weak as her only food had been the palm tree's fruit and bark. Crew members aboard a trawler [a kind of fishing boat] saw Melawati in her badly torn clothes, waving at them. They helped her climb aboard and took her to a hospital on Malaysia's Penang island. The crew said Melawati cried throughout her three days aboard the trawler."

The Sydney Morning Herald [Australia]

STEVE HUNTER'S STORY

Steve Hunter, from the United Kingdom, was working as a deep-sea diver on Phi Phi Island off the coast of Thailand. He was still in bed when the tsunami struck. The story of what happens begins in the panel below.

▶ "IT SOUNDED LIKE THUNDER"

"It was the noise that woke me. It sounded like thunder and falling water. I ran to the window to look outside. Down in the street I could see water. It was just a trickle at first—crawling through the dust. Just then a crack ripped through the door with a loud splintering of wood. The door burst open as if it had been kicked in. Water crashed into the room and pinned me against the wall. I could only gasp for breath before the wall fell down all around me and I blacked out.

When I woke I was treading water, but I had no idea where I was. It was dark and my head was banging on a concrete ceiling. The water was rising even higher. I sucked in some air and dived down to a hole between jagged bricks. Suddenly, I was carried along in a gush of water and found myself outside. There was blood and a huge gash at my ankle. It looked as if a sheet of iron from the roof had sliced through my leg. I didn't think I was going to survive."

Steve Hunter was incredibly lucky to survive the disaster.

Steve Hunter's leg took many months to heal. This picture was taken nine months after the disaster.

Steve pulled himself up a hillside to get above the swirling water. He scrambled into a hut, where other shocked people were taking shelter. Someone looked at his ripped ankle and poured alcohol on it to kill any germs from the dirty water. He screamed in pain and lay awake all night, hoping for help to arrive. The next day some men carried Steve outside and at last a helicopter rushed him to the hospital. His ankle was badly wounded and he had lost a lot of blood.

After surgery he was flown to Bangkok Hospital for further treatment. It took over a year and many operations before Steve could walk well again. But he had been lucky. The night before the tsunami struck, he had been staying in a hut on the beach. The wave washed away the hut and all the people staying there. "I'm so lucky to be alive," he said. "My friends were killed, but I survived."

UNDER THE RUBBLE

Can you imagine being buried alive for two weeks? A 60-year-old man named Sirasena was found under the rubble of Galle in Sri Lanka. He was only able to mumble his name and that he had a son and daughter. Sirasena was very weak and had a broken arm. By the state of his body, doctors could tell he had been under the rubble for almost two weeks. He probably stayed alive by drinking rainwater.

A month after the disaster, there seemed to be no chance of any more missing people being found. But then came more good news. A police party found five men, three children, and one woman in a remote part of Campbell Bay, an island in the Indian Ocean. They had been there for 38 days. The weak survivors said they had been swept into the sea by the wave and were later thrown back on to the beach. They survived by eating coconuts, and kept hoping someone would find them. Their hope paid off.

Many people were buried under rubble when houses and other buildings collapsed.

Tsunami was born just a few hours after the waves struck.

Hours after fleeing her home on an island in the Indian Ocean, Namita Roy gave birth on a jungle hilltop. She and her husband had to wait there with 700 other survivors. They ate bananas and drank coconut milk for days before help arrived. Both mother and baby survived. The baby's name will always remind them of their survival story. He was named Tsunami.

People from over 50 countries were killed by the tsunami. These included over 250 people from Australia, over 150 from the United Kingdom, and over 50 from the United States. But many tourists had lucky escapes.

A LUCKY ESCAPE

"We were out at sea in an 26-foot-long boat that was going from Thailand to a small island when we saw the tsunami. We were about half a mile from shore when the boat driver very quickly headed for a nearby bay. We had enough time to plan for when we hit the beach. It was a very close call and we made it to shore with only about ten seconds to spare. We ran to higher ground. We are thankful to say we have nothing more to show for it than just a few scratches."

Jason and Lisa Bagby, email to CNN

THE WORLD RESPONDS

The Asian Tsunami, 2004

TO THE RESCUE

As more and more news reached the world's television screens, people began to realize the scale of the disaster.

Hundreds of thousands of people needed help immediately. They needed food, clean water, blankets, shelter, and medical supplies. They needed workers to organize and deliver these supplies, and to take care of all the injured. The **United Nations** described this as the largest aid operation in the history of the world.

Relief organizations got to work right away. Ships and planes full of materials for setting up camps were sent to the countries hit by the tsunami. Even with such a fast response, it took days before supplies reached some of the remote places. The waves had washed away many roads and bridges. Some villages could only be reached by helicopter.

Helicopters were used to bring emergency food and water supplies to survivors in hard-to-reach places.

A RACE AGAINST TIME

One of the first tasks was to recover the dead bodies. It was impossible to identify them all before they had to be buried. Even two months later, 500 bodies were still being found each day in Indonesia.

The risk of disease was a real problem. With the water supply contaminated, there was a danger that weak survivors could become ill. It was feared that **cholera** could cause more deaths than the tsunami itself.

Mosquitoes soon came to breed in the many large areas of **stagnant** water left after the floods. Mosquitoes spread **malaria**. Relief teams had to work fast to drain flooded areas and to bring in tanks of fresh water.

PEOPLE'S RESPONSES

People from all over the world were shocked by the scenes of devastation shown on television. They responded with gifts and fund-raising events. People and organizations raised over $400 million in just a few days.

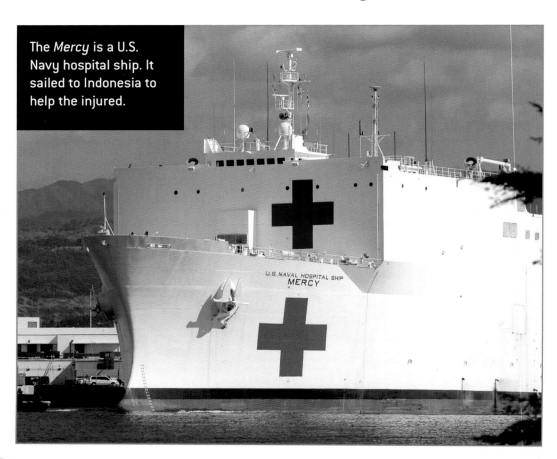

The *Mercy* is a U.S. Navy hospital ship. It sailed to Indonesia to help the injured.

U.S. NAVAL HOSPITAL SHIP
MERCY

Trained dogs and elephants were used in some search-and-rescue operations. Dogs were used to detect dead bodies under piles of debris or in waterlogged areas. Elephants then lifted away heavy pieces of wood or concrete so that rescuers could retrieve the bodies.

A huge problem was tending to all the wounded. People with serious injuries were taken by helicopter to the crowded city hospitals. But many people living in the camps had scratches that became infected. Medical teams had to work fast to treat these infections.

Around 150 small camps sprung up within a week in Aceh, Sumatra. Relief workers encouraged all healthy people to work together to clear the debris. "The damage is mind-boggling, but they are rebuilding and everybody is moving around with a purpose," one of the doctors reported.

Camps set up for homeless people are often called refugee camps. The word *refugee* usually refers to someone who seeks shelter or a home for some reason. When reading about disasters, you might come across the term *IDS* instead. *IDS* stands for "Internally Displaced Persons."

WITHIN WEEKS

Countries around the world promised to send money, workers, and equipment to rebuild areas hit by the tsunami. Governments from 87 countries gave over $5 billion in total.

Ships from the United States arrived in the disaster zones carrying supplies, thousands of troops, and about 50 helicopters. Other ships arrived that could turn seawater into clean drinking water. The United States also sent $2 billion for relief work.

People in Great Britain began giving money at the rate of $1.75 million an hour. After just a few weeks, the public had raised $620 million. The British government sent $130 million to help the rescue effort, as well as ships and helicopters.

The Australian public raised over $220 million, and the government sent over $1 billion. Australia also sent ships and airplanes to help.

FEBRUARY 2005

Leaders from around the world visited the disaster areas. They saw for themselves what needed to be done and helped to arrange more relief efforts. Two former U.S. presidents toured camps and encouraged Americans to give more money. Bill Clinton and George Bush, Sr., spoke to the world about what they saw.

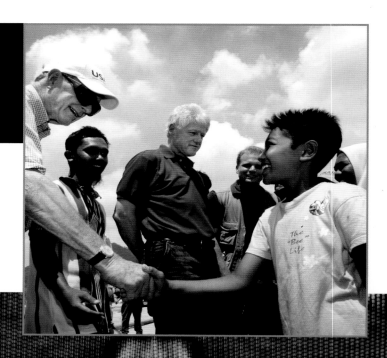

Former presidents George H. W. Bush and Bill Clinton helped to raise money for the relief effort.

Doctors in the Singapore Army performed medical checks in temporary clinics in Sumatra.

Giving money was one thing, but making sure it got to the right places was a difficult task. The first question facing everyone was: Where to start? It was vital for rescue teams to make an impact quickly. If survivors did not see help arriving soon, they would lose all hope. During the first few weeks after the tsunami, rescue work included providing emotional support as well as food, water, and medicine.

Singapore was close to the **epicenter** of the earthquake on December 26. However, it was sheltered from the tsunami by the island of Sumatra. Being close to the devastation of Sumatra, Singapore was able to get large rescue ships to the scene very quickly. The Singapore Armed Forces (SAF) organized its biggest-ever rescue, named Operation Flying Eagle. The SAF field hospitals in Meulaboh and Banda Aceh treated over 5,000 patients. Warships carried 210 tons of relief supplies, and SAF helicopters transported relief supplies and thousands of rescued people.

MONTHS LATER

Months after the tsunami struck, thousands of people were still living in camps. Some people had to sleep in the hallways of public buildings or anywhere they could find that gave shelter from rain.

There was **criticism** that the relief work took so long. But the scale and difficulty of the rebuilding needed a huge effort. No operation had been done on such a large scale before.

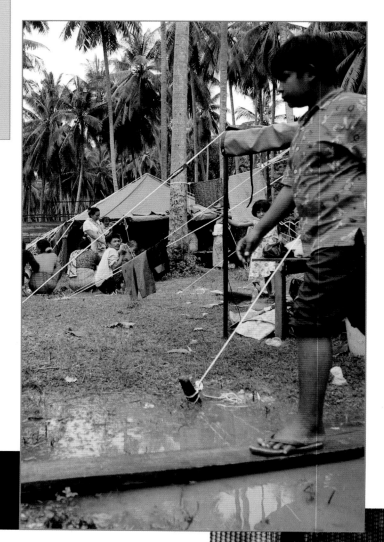

Many camps were still overcrowded six months after the disaster.

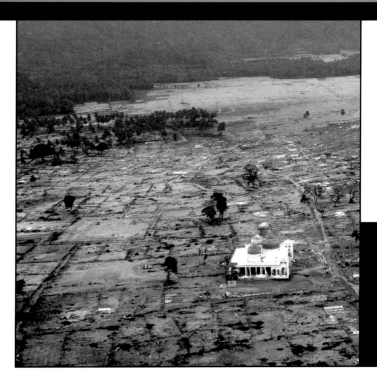

The Grand Mosque was one of the few buildings in Banda Aceh to remain standing after the waves hit.

All the planning and shipping of building materials, bulldozers, and cranes took a long time. The tsunami had also killed many skilled workers, so people had to be trained as builders.

Only when all the debris had been searched and cleared could the job of rebuilding begin. Slowly the shattered villages, towns, roads, pipes, and cables are being put back together. The work will take many years to finish.

> ### ▷ SIX MONTHS LATER
>
> "We're talking about 180,000 houses that have to be rebuilt. The size and scale of the debris is simply still unbelievable [...] Just clearing away so much after six months has been a Herculean effort."
>
> Tim Costello, World Vision Australia Chief Executive, speaking in June 2005

CHILDREN OF THE TSUNAMI

The Asian Tsunami, 2004

A DISASTER OF THE YOUNG

When disaster struck in the Indian Ocean in December 2004, millions of lives would never be the same again.

The tsunami changed the lives of many children forever. Thousands of children lost their families and their homes. Many were badly injured. It is estimated that 40 percent of the dead were young children and babies. They were less able to run away, swim, or climb trees. They were also victims of disease in the days that followed. Even so, many children did manage to climb palm trees or run to higher ground. Some babies were found alive, floating on mattresses from their beds.

Despite all the survival stories, it was thought the tsunami left about 1.5 million children homeless. Many of the children were left **orphaned**.

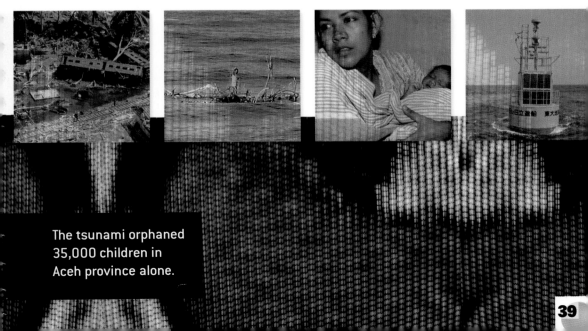

The tsunami orphaned 35,000 children in Aceh province alone.

ORPHANS OF THE WAVES

The charity Save the Children organized toys, clothes, and medical supplies for the 35 children at this orphanage in Sri Lanka.

Once the waves had retreated, people were left confused, lost, and stunned. Children wandered through the rubble, trying to find anyone they knew. Some were lucky and found their families, but many others did not. It took months for relief workers to help children and their parents find each other. They had to find homes for the many orphans who had nowhere to go.

Children affected by the tsunami needed more than just shelter, medicine, and food. The **trauma** they had suffered left many young people in need of **counseling**. Children's charities tried to give emotional support to all those suffering from loss, grief, stress, and fear. It was important to help children feel secure again. Charities helped them get back to school. There they could play, learn, and talk about what had happened.

Although many schools had been washed away or used as shelters for the homeless, new schools were set up again. Some children will need help and support for many years.

TSUNAMI FLY HIGH!

Exactly three months after the tsunami struck, 27 orphaned children were given the ride of their lives. The Indian Air Force took each child for a flight in a microlight aircraft. The first child to go up was Reshmita. As she flew off in the plane, the other children on the ground waved and cheered. When she landed she giggled, "I am going to be a pilot!"

Helpers organized games, such as volleyball, to help children overcome the trauma they had suffered.

FOUND

Among all the tragic stories of parents or children being lost forever, there were some stories with happy endings.

After over six months apart, a father and daughter found each other again. Just before the tsunami struck, Muhamed Ali's sixteen-year-old daughter, Handayani, went to visit an aunt in the coastal town of Meulaboh, Sumatra. When the tsunami struck, Handayani disappeared and her father did not know if she was still alive. He moved to a camp after his wife and house were washed away. As time went by, there was no word of his missing daughter, and he feared the worst.

U.S. landing craft vehicles delivered supplies to the people of Meulaboh, on the island of Sumatra. The vehicles can transport more supplies than helicopters in a single trip.

In fact she had survived and been taken to another camp. Several months later government workers asked about Handayani's family. They traced her father and arranged to take her to him. When they met up again, they could not believe their eyes. "I thought she was dead," Muhamed Ali said. "This is amazing!"

BOY IS REUNITED WITH FATHER IN THAILAND

A weeping father found his missing two-year-old son, Hannes, days after the tsunami. The family was on vacation from Sweden when the disaster struck. Someone found the small boy sitting alone on a roadside and took him to a hospital. Workers at the hospital posted his photo on the Internet to try to find his family. His uncle happened to see the photo and rushed to claim Hannes, whose father was in another hospital. At last father and son were brought together again. "I couldn't survive if I lost them both," the man said, telling how his wife had been dragged away by the wave.

The Internet helped to reunite this father with his son.

TIMELINE

Sunday, December 26, 2004, local time:
7:59 A.M. (Dec. 25, 7:59 P.M. EST):

> An earthquake measuring 9 on the Richter scale is recorded off the coast of Sumatra, Indonesia. Buildings shake in Bangkok, Thailand, around 780 miles (1,260 kilometers) away, as well as in Singapore, 590 miles (950 kilometers) away. Several strong **aftershocks** follow.

8:30 A.M. (Dec. 25, 8:30 P.M. EST):

> The first waves strike Sumatra in Indonesia.

9:30 A.M. (Dec. 25, 9:30 P.M. EST):

> The waves reach Thailand.

9:00 A.M. (Dec. 25, 10:00 P.M. EST):

> Southern India and Sri Lanka are hit by the waves.

9:30 A.M. (Dec. 25, 11:30 P.M. EST):

> The Maldives are flooded by the tsunami.

11:12 A.M. (Dec. 26, 12:12 A.M. EST):

> 150 people are reported dead in Sri Lanka. Within 30 minutes, the figure reaches 3,000.

10:00 to 11:00 A.M. (Dec. 26, 2:00 to 3:00 A.M. EST):

> The waves reach East Africa.

Monday, December 27:

> A massive rescue operation begins. The estimated death toll reaches 26,000, with at least 12,000 in Sri Lanka alone.

Tuesday, December 28:

The death toll rises to 60,000. Mass burials of bodies begin.

Wednesday, December 29:

The death toll is predicted to exceed 100,000. The confirmed figure rises to 77,000.

Thursday, December 30:

The death toll approaches 120,000.

Friday, December 31:

The United Nations warns the tsunami death toll could reach 150,000.

January 19, 2005:

The death toll in Indonesia alone nearly doubles to more than 166,000. This is later revised to about 130,000. Media reports say worldwide deaths stand at more than 250,000.

December 26, 2005:

Millions of people take part in ceremonies to mark the first anniversary of the disaster.

INDEX